SIMPLY SCIENCE

Fall

by Darlene R. Stille

Content Advisers: Terrence E. Young Jr., M.Ed., M.L.S.,
Jefferson Parish (La.) Public Schools, and Janann Jenner, Ph.D.

Reading Adviser: Dr. Linda D. Labbo,
Department of Reading Education, College of Education,
The University of Georgia

 COMPASS POINT BOOKS

Minneapolis, Minnesota

Compass Point Books
3722 West 50th Street, #115
Minneapolis, MN 55410

Visit Compass Point Books on the Internet at *www.compasspointbooks.com* or e-mail your request to *custserv@compasspointbooks.com*

Photographs ©:

International Stock/Wayne Aldridge, cover; Leslie O'Shaughnessy, 4; Cheryl A. Ertelt, 5, 11; Photo Network/Gay Bumgarner, 6, 18; Richard Hamilton Smith, 7, 23, 25; Stephen J. Lang/Visuals Unlimited, 8; Dominique Braud/Tom Stack and Associates, 10; Rob and Ann Simpson, 12; Photo Network, Chad Ehlers, 13; John D. Cunningham/Visuals Unlimited, 14; Jeff March, 15, 28; David Jensen, 16; Inga Spence/Tom Stack and Associates, 17; Kent and Donna Dannen, 19, 29; D. Cavagnaro/Visuals Unlimited, 20; NASA/TSADO/Tom Stack and Associates, 22; Marilyn Moseley LaMantia, 24; Unicorn Stock Photos/Kathi Corder, 27.

Editors: E. Russell Primm, Emily J. Dolbear, and Melissa Stewart
Photo Researcher: Svetlana Zhurkina
Photo Selector: Matthew Eisentrager-Warner
Designer: Bradfordesign, Inc.

Library of Congress Cataloging-in-Publication Data

Stille, Darlene R.
    Fall / by Darlene Stille.
        p. cm. — (Simply science)
    Includes bibliographical references and index.
    ISBN 0-7565-0093-1(hardcover : lib. bdg.)
        1. Autumn—Juvenile literature. [1. Autumn.] I. Title. II. Simply science (Minneapolis, Minn.)
    QB637.7 .S75 2001
    508.2—dc21   00-011000

Table of Contents

Signs of Fall 5

Animals in the Fall 7

Fall Colors 13

Harvest Time 17

A Harvest Moon 22

The Days Grow Shorter 28

Glossary 30

Did You Know? 30

Want to Know More? 31

Index 32

Signs of Fall

As you walk to the bus stop one morning, you notice that the air seems cooler. Soon you will need to start wearing a coat. A few weeks later, you see that the leaves are changing color. Some have already fallen to the ground. When you step on the leaves, you hear them crunch. It's fall.

Fall is one of the four seasons of the year.

Leaves changing color means fall is near.

Playing in fall leaves ▶

It is also called **autumn**. Fall comes after summer and before winter. In North America, fall begins around September 21 and lasts until around December 21.

Signs of fall are easy to spot.

Squirrels store food they gather during the fall.

Animals in the Fall

Have you ever watched squirrels gather seeds and nuts in the fall? As soon as they find a seed or a nut, they run off to hide it. They are storing food in the fall, so that they will have something to eat during the winter.

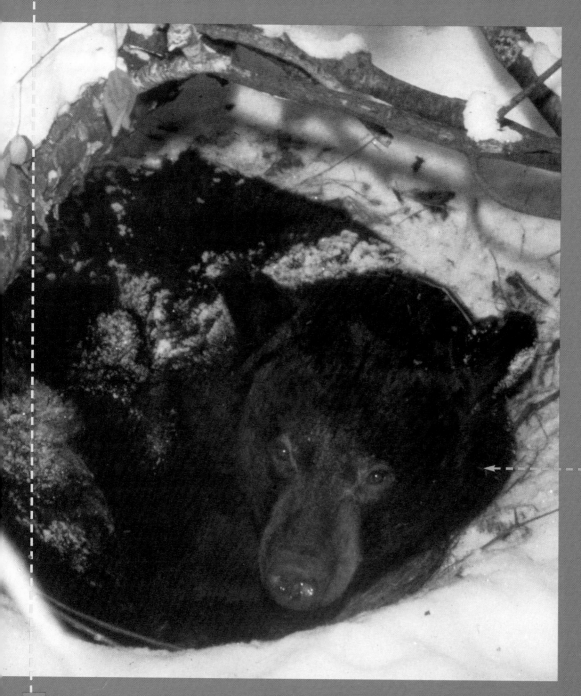

Many other animals eat lots of food in the fall to prepare for winter. That helps them build up a layer of fat in their bodies. During winter, they sleep most of the time. Bears sleep during winter. They get the energy they need from the fat they stored in their bodies.

Chipmunks and squirrels also sleep most of the winter. But sometimes they wake up and eat the seeds and nuts they stored during fall.

Some birds sleep during the winter. Snakes and frogs are also animals that go into winter sleep.

A black bear sleeps most of the time during the winter.

Many animals stay active all winter. They grow thick, heavy coats in the fall. Dogs grow extra hair to keep them warm all winter long. When spring comes, dogs shed their winter fur.

Some birds and insects **migrate** in the fall. They fly to warmer places. Ducks and geese fly south in large flocks. These birds form a V-shaped pattern in the sky.

◀ *Migrating Canada geese*

Dogs grow extra hair in fall ▶
to help keep them warm.

Fall Colors

Have you ever wondered why the leaves on many trees turn red or orange or yellow in the fall? Those colors were there all the time. During the summer, those colors were covered up by the leaves' green color.

The green color comes from tiny parts of the leaf that

Fall colors can help make things more beautiful.

Some of the bright colors of fall ▶

collect sunlight and make food for the tree. When the days grow cooler, the leaves stop making food. Soon, their green color fades away and you can see the other colors.

◀ Maple leaves in the sun

Leaves lose their green ▶
color in the fall.

Harvest Time

Trees are not the only plants that go through changes in the fall. Flowers stop blooming, and grasses start to turn brown. Most plants have stopped growing for the year.

In September, farmers **harvest** most of their crops. They store corn to feed their pigs and cows in the

The countryside turns brown in autumn.

A farmer harvesting wheat ▶

winter. They cut their wheat and sell it. Bakers use the wheat to make delicious bread. Your breakfast cereal may also be made from wheat.

By October, pumpkins are big and fat. They are ready to be picked. Some people like to make pies with these orange vegetables. It's fun to carve a face in a pumpkin at Halloween.

Fruits and squash are common in the fall.

Pumpkin carving ▶

Some gourds and squashes also ripen in the fall. Colorful gourds make great decorations. You can bake squashes and eat them.

Fruit farmers pick apples from trees in the fall. Some of the apples are sold. Some are crushed to make apple cider.

In November, people in the United States celebrate Thanksgiving. They give thanks for a good harvest. In Canada, people celebrate Thanksgiving in October.

Fruit farmers pressing apples to make cider

A Harvest Moon

Have you ever noticed that the moon looks very big and bright on an autumn night? People call this a **harvest moon**. The full moon closest to the first day of fall is the harvest moon.

The harvest moon lights up the night sky, so that farmers can work late at night. They can see well enough to harvest their crops.

A harvest moon

Farmers working in the harvest moon's light

You probably know that the moon does not always look the same. Sometimes you can't see the moon at all. Then, a few nights later, the moon looks like a tiny slice of silver. We call it a "new moon."

As the days pass, the moon seems to grow bigger and rounder. But the moon does not really change shape.

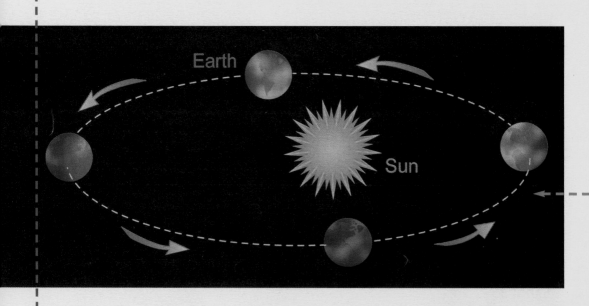

Just as Earth travels around the sun once each year, the moon **orbits** Earth about once each month. It takes Earth about 365 days to travel around the sun. It takes the moon about twenty-seven days to travel around Earth.

As the moon orbits Earth, we see different parts of it. Some nights, we see a full moon.

On other nights, we see just half a

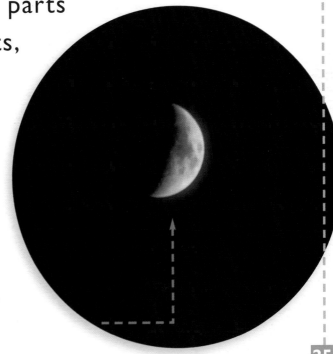

Just as Earth moves around the sun, the moon moves around Earth.

The moon seems to take different shapes during the month.

moon. That's because we can see only the part of the moon that is lit up by the sun. The moon has no light of its own. The brightness you see when you look at the moon comes from the sun. Sunlight is **reflected** by the moon. And of course, the sun lights up different parts of the moon as the moon travels around Earth.

Less daylight means less time to play outside.

The Days Grow Shorter

You can find the shortest day of the year by looking at a clock. A clock shows the hours and minutes in a day. There are twenty-four hours in one day. On the first day of fall, there are

exactly twelve hours of daylight and twelve hours of darkness. After that, each day has fewer hours of daylight and more hours of darkness.

You can observe this change and keep a record of it in a notebook. Each day, when the sun is setting, look at a clock. During the fall, you will see that the sun sets a little earlier each day. On the shortest day of the year, fall ends and winter begins.

The amounts of daylight and darkness are the same on the first day of fall.

A fall sunset ▶

Glossary

autumn—fall

harvest—to pick and gather crops

harvest moon—the first full moon after fall has begun

migrate—to travel to warmer parts of the world to find food or have young

orbit—to move around or circle

reflected—bounced off

Did You Know?

- During the late summer and fall, hurricanes sometimes form over the ocean and come onto land. Hurricanes are violent storms. They have strong winds and heavy rains. Some hurricanes destroy boats, houses, and roads.

- Some flowers bloom only in the fall.

- If you do not rake the leaves in your yard, most of them will rot during the winter. But oak leaves have a waxy coating. They take a very long time to rot.

Want to Know More?

At the Library

Ross, Kathy, and Vicky Enright (illustrator). *Crafts to Make in the Fall*. Brookfield, Conn.:
Millbrook Press, 1999.

Sipiera, Paul P., and Diane M. Sipiera. *Seasons*. Danbury, Conn.: Children's Press, 1998.

Supraner, Robyn. *I Can Read about Seasons*. Mawah, N.J.: Troll, 1999.

On the Web

Crafts for Kids

http://craftsforkids.about.com/parenting/craftsforkids

For dozens of craft projects related to the current season

Through the Mail

Farmers' Almanac Order Desk

P.O. Box 1609

Mount Hope Avenue

Lewiston, ME 04241

To order a seasonal guide with long-range weather forecasts

On the Road

Fall Foliage in New England

http://www.7almanac.com/articles/fall.html

To find out when the autumn leaves are most colorful in each New England state

Index

air, 5
animals, 7, 9–10
apples, 21
autumn, 6, 30
birds, 10
clocks, 28
color, 13–14
daylight, 28–29
dogs, 10
ducks, 10
farmers, 17, 21–22
fruit, 21
geese, 10
gourds, 21
harvest, 17, 30
harvest moon, 22, 30

leaves, 5, 13–14
migration, 10, 30
moon, 22, 24–26
new moon, 24
orbit, 25, 30
plants, 17
pumpkins, 18
reflection, 26, 30
seasons, 5
squash, 21
squirrels, 7
sun, 26, 29
Thanksgiving, 21
wheat, 18
winter, 29
winter sleep, 9

About the Author

Darlene R. Stille is a science editor and writer. She has lived in Chicago, Illinois, all her life. When she was in high school, she fell in love with science. While attending the University of Illinois, she discovered that she also enjoyed writing. Today she feels fortunate to have a career that allows her to pursue both her interests. Darlene R. Stille has written more than thirty books for young people.